Science Experiments For Kids

49 Cool Kids Science Experiments

JB Publishing Ltd 2017

All rights reserved. No part of this publication may be reproduced, distributed, or transmitted in any form by any means, including photocopying, recording, or other electronic or mechanical methods, without the prior written permission of the publisher, except in the case of brief quotations embodied in critical reviews and certain other commercial uses permitted by copyright law.

Adult supervision is required at all times during the practice and performance of each science experiment. The information in this book is for informational purposes only, no liability for illness or injury resulting from the contents of this book is taken by the author.

FLOATING EGG IN SALT WATER

To perform this experiment, you will need an egg, salt, some water and 2x clear glasses.

Step by step
1. Pour some water in the glass (half fill glass)
2. Put some salt in the water (5 spoons)
3. Pour more water in the glass (almost fill glass)
4. Put the egg in the water

Explanation
Because the salt water is denser than the normal water the egg floats in it. When you put the egg in the water it sinks through the normal water but stops when it reaches the salted water. If you didn't mix the ordinary water and the salt water the egg will float in the middle of the glass.

SPOON REFLECTION

To perform the experiment, you need a spoon.

Step by step
1. Pick up the spoon
2. Look at your reflection on the inside of the spoon
3. Look at your reflection on the back of the spoon

Explanation
When you look at your reflection on the inside of the spoon you see yourself larger, because the inside of the spoon is concave. When you look at your reflection on the back of the spoon you see yourself like you are farther away. That is because the back of the spoon is convex.

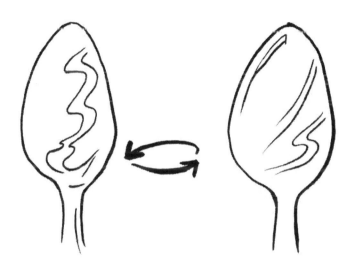

ENERGY TRANSFER THROUGH BALLS

To perform the experiment you need a big ball (basketball) and a small ball (tennis ball).

Step by step
1. Put the tennis ball on the top of the basketball
2. Hold one hand on the top of the tennis ball and one hand under the basketball
3. Let go of both of the balls (at the same time)

Explanation
Because the energy is transferring between the objects (in this case between the balls) the tennis ball will bounce off the basketball very high up in the air. The basketball will transfer its energy to the much smaller tennis ball and because of that energy the tennis ball will make a much higher bounce then normal.

MELTING CHOCOLATE

To perform the experiment, you need chocolate (small pieces of the same size), pen, paper and paper plates.

Step by step
1. Put a piece of a chocolate on a paper plate
2. Put the paper plate outside (in the shade)
3. Record how much time it takes for chocolate to melt
4. Repeat the experiment with putting the plate on other different places

Explanation
The purpose of the experiment id to see how fast the chocolate will melt under different conditions. The time of the melting will not be the same if you put the chocolate under the sun, in the shade or in your mouth. Also the time of melting will not be the same if you are doing the experiment with dark chocolate or white chocolate. Do the experiments, write down the results and compare them with each other.

STEEL WOOL & VINEGAR

To perform the experiment, you need some steel wool, vinegar, two beakers, thermometer and paper.

Step by step
1. Place the steel wool in a beaker
2. Pour vinegar on the steel wool
3. Wait a minute
4. Remove the steel wool
5. Dry out any remained vinegar
6. Wrap the steel wool around the base of the thermometer
7. Put the steel wool with the thermometer in the other beaker
8. Cover the beaker with paper
9. Make a hole in the paper to observe the thermometer
10. Check the starting temperature
11. Check the temperature every 5 minutes

Explanation

Because of the chemical reaction between the steel wool and the vinegar you will see how the steel wool is rusting in front of you. When you soak the steel wool in the vinegar you remove the protective coating of the steel wool and the iron in the steel begins to rust. The reaction creates heat energy which will increase the temperature in the beaker.

UNDERWATER PAPER

To perform the experiment, you need a bowl, water, paper and a glass.

Step by step
1. Fill the bowl with a water
2. Crumple up a sheet of paper
3. Put the paper on the bottom of the glass
4. Turn the glass upside down
5. Put the glass vertically into the bowl with water

Explanation
Because of the air in the glass the water can't reach the paper. When you put the glass into the water, the air in the glass has no space to move so it stays compressed in the glass and prevents the paper from getting wet.

MIXING OIL AND WATER

To perform the experiment, you will need a bottle, a glass of water, food coloring, cooking oil and dish detergent.

Step by step
1. Add a few drops of food coloring into the water
2. Pour some colored water (2 tablespoons) and some cooking oil (2 tablespoons) into the bottle
3. Shake the bottle
4. Put the bottle down

Explanation
Because the oil has a lower density than the water it will float above the water no matter how hard you mix them. You can mix them or shake them as hard as you want but at the end they will always separate one from another.

BENDING WATER WITH STATIC

To perform the experiment, you need a baloon and a water pipe.

Step by step
1. Turn on the water pipe so it falls down in a narrow stream
2. Rub the baloon to your hair
3. Now move the baloon close to the water

Explanation
Because of the static electricity that is on the balloon it will bend the stream of water when you put the balloon near it. With rubbing the balloon to your hair you charge it with a static electricity (negatively charged particles), so when you put the balloon near the water it attracts the water (positively charged particles) towards itself and the stream bends.

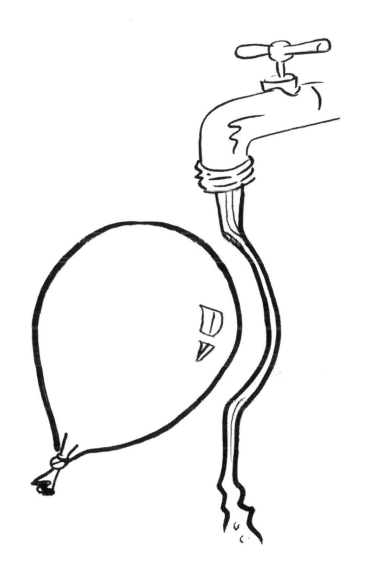

MAKE YOUR OWN QUICKSAND

To perform the experiment, you will need a glass of water, large plastic container, cup of maize corn flour and a spoon.

Step by step
1. Put the water in the container
2. Put the corn flour in the water
3. Mix the water and the corn flour (to make an instant sand)
4. Stir it at the right speed (not too quick because the sand will become hard)
5. Pock the quicksand

Explanation
The water and the corn flour make a perfect combination to demonstrate how quicksand works. With mixing the water and corn flour you can understand how quicksand is responding to slow or quick stirring and to slow or fast poking. If you stir or poke fast the quicksand becomes hard, if you stir or poke slow the quicksand is much more permeable.

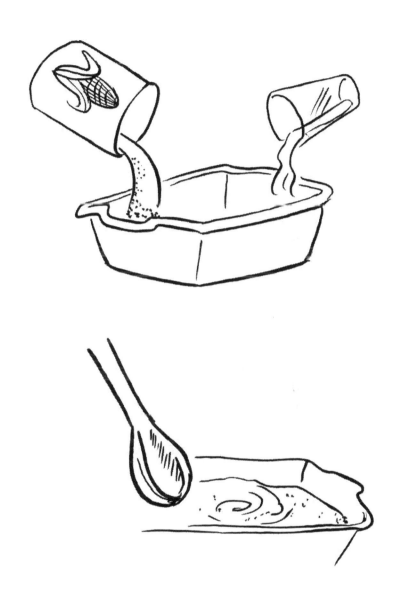

WARM AIR NEEDS MORE ROOM

To perform the experiment, you need an empty glass bottle, balloon and a pot of hot water. Make sure to have an adult helping you!

Step by step
1. Put the balloon on the mouth of the bottle
2. Put the bottle in the pot of hot water (not boiling water)
3. Wait a few minutes

Explanation
Because the warm air takes up more space than the cold air the balloon will start to inflate when you put the glass bottle with the balloon on it to the hot water. The amount of the air in the balloon is the same as at the beginning of the experiment, it is because the air in it is getting warmer, so it needs more space to expand.

JUMPING COIN

To perform the experiment, you will need cold water, ice cubes, a glass bowl and a coin.

Step by step
1. Fill the bowl with a cold water
2. Put the bottle under the bowl
3. Put the ice cubes in the bowl
4. Wait a few minutes
5. Place a coin to the top of the bottle
6. Wrap your hands around the bottle
7. Wait a few seconds

Explanation
Because of the difference of the temperature inside and outside the bottle you can make a coin jump. When you wrap your hands around the bottle you heat up the air inside it. This warm air pushes harder than the cold air outside the bottle so it forces the coin to up.

BAKING SODA & VINEGAR VOLCANO

To perform the experiment you need a vinegar, baking soda, paper towels and a container.

Step by step
1. Put some of the baking soda in the container
2. Pour some vinegar onto the baking soda
3. Wait a few minutes

Explanation
Because of the reaction between the baking soda and the vinegar it will look like a volcano exploding in the room. The soda is a base and the vinegar is an acid. When you put those two together you create a reaction in which then forms carbonic acid. It is very unstable, so at the same moment it breaks apart into water and carbon dioxide, which gives you the effect of a volcano erupting.

EGG BUBBLES

To perform the experiment you need an egg, glass of hot water, clear glass and a magnifying glass. Make sure to get an adult to help you with this experiment!

Step by step
1. Put the egg in the glass
2. Pour the hot water in the glass over the egg (until the glass is almost full)
3. Wait a few minutes
4. Use your magnifying glass to observe what happens with the egg

Explanation
Because of the hot water the egg will release a lot of small air bubbles. The egg's shell contains a lot of small holes called pores. Under the shell there is an air pocket which protects the egg from cracking. When you put the egg in the hot water the air in that air pocket starts to expand and is trying to find its way out. It goes out through the pores hence the bubbles.

RAW OR BOILED EGG?

To perform the experiment you need one raw egg and one hard-boiled egg (it has to be the same temperature than the raw egg so let it cool first). Make sure to get an adult to boil the egg for you!

Step by step
1. Spin the raw egg
2. Spin the hard-boiled egg
3. Observe the difference in the time of spinning

Explanation
Because of the difference in what is inside of the eggs the raw egg is spinning much longer than the hard-boiled egg. The yolk in the raw egg is free to move so when you spin it it gets a different kind of force than the yolk in the hard-boiled egg, which is positioned in one place and cannot move.

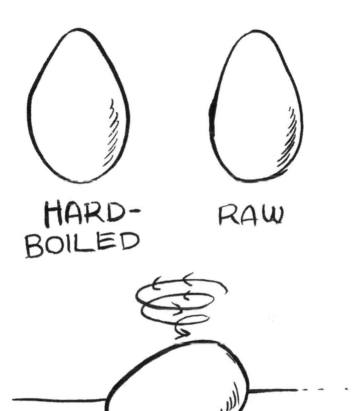

MAKE A RAINBOW

To perform the experiment you need a glass of water and a piece of paper.

Step by step
1. Find a room with sunlight in it
2. Hold the glass over the paper so the sunlight goes through the water onto the paper
3. Try to move the glass around so the heights and angles of the glass on the paper vary

Explanation
Because the sunlight bends as it passes through the water you can make a rainbow in your room. It is the same procedure like with the natural rainbow, where the sunlight bends through the raindrops. Here you change the raindrops with a glass of water and you can make a rainbow at home. As you move the glass to different heights and angles you highlight different colors.

GLOWING WATER

To perform the experiment you need a blue light, highlighter pen and a little water.

Step by step
1. Open the highlighter pen
2. Soak the pen into the water
3. Wait a few minutes
4. Go in the dark room
5. Turn on the blue light
6. Brighten the water in which was the highlighter pen

Explanation
Because of the structure of the water, highlighter pen and a blue light you can make the water glow. The highlighter pen contains phosphors and when you soak it in the water some of the phosphors go into it. The phosphors can turn the blue light (UV light which we can't see with our own eyes) into a visible light. When you brighten the water with the blue light you can see the phosphors in it and it looks like the water is glowing.

BEND A STRAW

To perform the experiment you need a straw and a glass of water.

Step by step
1. Put the straw in the glass with the water
2. Look at the straw from the top and bottom of the glass
3. Look at the straw from the side of the glass (focus on the point where the straw enters the water)

Explanation
Because the light changes the direction when it goes through the water we see things differently when we look at things through the water. When you look at the straw on the point where it enters the water you see the upper part of it normally through the air and it is straight, but the lower part you see through the water and because the light bends in the water you see the straw under a different angle, so it seems like the straw is bent.

FLOATING M&M'S

To perform the experiment you need a glass, water and a few M&M's.

Step by step
1. Place the M&M's on the bottom of the bowl ("M" facing up)
2. Pour in the bowl around 4 centimeters of water
3. Wait a few minutes

Explanation
Because the letter M is printed in edible white ink it will not dissolve in the water like the rest of the candy. The letter will peel off and float to the top, rest of the M&M's will vanish in the water.

BATH SALTS

To perform the experiment you need a bowl, rolling pin, plastic bag, spoon, essential oil, washing soda and food coloring.

Step by step
1. Put one cup of washing soda into the plastic bag
2. Crush the lumps of soda with a rolling pin
3. Empty the bag in a bowl
4. Pour some essential oil in the bowl
5. Stir a few drops of food coloring in the bowl
6. Pour the mixture in the batch full of water

Explanation
Because of the chemical structure of all the elements you put in the mixture for making bath salts you get a relaxing and refreshing bath for you or for somebody you care about.

MICROSCOPIC CREATURES IN WATER

To perform the experiment you need a microscope, concave slide, dropper and water (many different samples of water from different places).

Step by step
1. Set up your microscope
2. Put some water on the concave slide (use the dropper)
3. Examine the water with the microscope
4. Try different samples

Explanation
Because the water structure is not the same at every place, you can compare what you find in the samples you took at from the different places. You can see which creatures are the same in every sample and which creatures are identifiable only in specific samples.

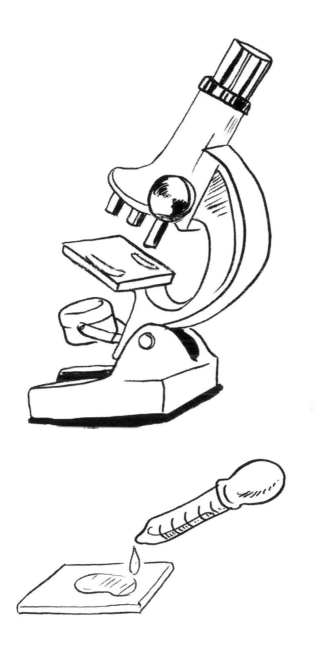

ESCAPING WATER

To perform the experiment you need a glass of water, paper towels and an empty glass.

Step by step
1. Twist a couple of paper towels together to form a piece of rope
2. Place one end of the rope in the glass with water (into the water) and one end of the rope in the empty glass
3. Wait a few minutes

Explanation
Because of the structure of the paper towels and the behavior of the water you can make the water go from one glass to another glass. This process is possible because the water can move along the tiny gasps in the fiber of the towels. After a few minutes into the experiments you will see that the empty glass will start to filling with the water from the full glass. This process is known as osmosis.

THE BOUNCY EGG

To perform the experiment you need a glass, vinegar and an egg.

Step by step
1. Pout the vinegar into the glass
2. Place the egg in the vinegar
3. Leave the egg in the vinegar for two days

Explanation
Because of the chemical reaction between the vinegar and eggshell the eggshell becomes soft and dissolves. You can throw it down on the floor and see if it will bounce up.

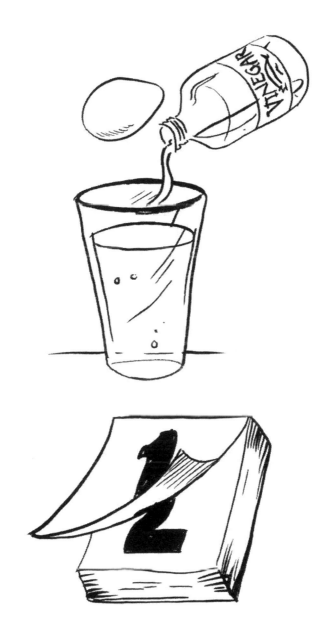

STAB A POTATO WITH A STRAW

To perform the experiment you need a raw potato and plastic straws.

Step by step
1. Take the straw holding it on the side
2. Try to stab the potato
3. Take another straw holding it on the side and placing your thumb over the top
4. Try to stab the potato

Explanation
Because your thumb has trapped the air in the straw you can now stab the potatoe. The difference between first attempt and second attempt is that when you put your thumb over the top of the straw in second attempt you trap the air that is inside the straw and the straw becomes strong enough to penetrate into the potato.

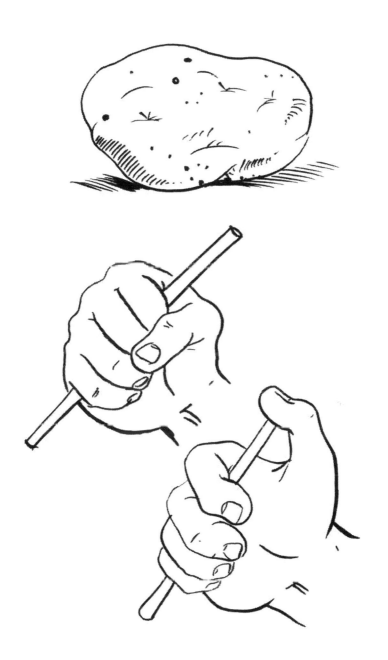

TASTE TESTING WITHOUT SMELL

To perform the experiment you need a piece of peeled apple and a piece of peeled potato. Remember to get an adult to peel these for you!

Step by step
1. Close your eyes
2. Mix the pieces of potato and apple
3. Hold your nose
4. Try to eat one piece
5. Try to eat the other piece
6. Tell which was which piece

Explanation
Your nose is for tasting food and is much important than your mouth for tasting. By holding your nose you take away a lot of your senses for food tasting, so you will have a lot of problems with telling the difference between the apple and the potato when you try them.

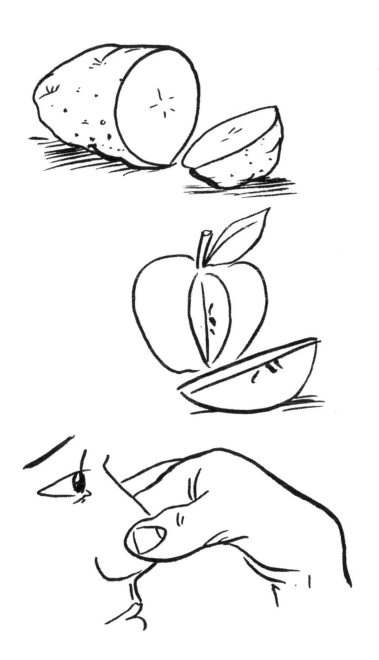

DISSOLVING SUGAR AT DIFFERENT HEATS

To perform the experiment you need sugar cubes, a glass of hot water, glass of cold water and a spoon.

Step by step
1. Equal the levels of hot water and cold water in the glasses
2. Put a sugar cube in the cold water
3. Stir the water until sugar disappears
4. Keep putting the sugar cubes in cold water until the sugar stops dissolving (when it starts to gather at the bottom of the glass it is not dissolving any more)
5. Write down how many sugar cubes you put in the cold water
6. Put sugar cube in the hot water
7. Stir the water until sugar disappears
8. Keep putting the sugar cubes in hot water until the sugar stops dissolving (when it starts to gather at the bottom of the glass it is not dissolving any more)
9. Compare the results

Explanation

Because of the difference in the temperatures of the water you will notice that you put various number of sugar cubes in the cold and hot water. The hot water can dissolve more sugar because it has faster moving molecules in it and they can process the dissolving better and faster than the molecules in the cold water.

PLANT SEEDS

To perform the experiment you need fresh pumpkin seeds, potting soil, a small container, light and some heat.

Step by step
1. Fil the container with the potting soil
2. Plant the pumpkin seed in the soil
3. Place the container somewhere warm, but no under direct sunlight
4. Dampen the soil on an everyday bases (do not use too much water)
5. Observe and record what is happening with the seeds

Explanation
Because you made the right conditions the seeds will grow up from the soil. This is called germination. It is a process of a plant emerging from a seed and beginning to grow. Observe your plants through a longer amount of time (a few weeks) and see how they are growing and developing.

MAKING MUSIC WITH WATER

To perform the experiment you need water, six glasses and a wooden stick.

Step by step
1. Put the glasses in one line
2. Fill the glasses with various amounts of water (first with the smallest amount, last with the biggest amount)
3. Hit the glasses with the wooden stick

Explanation
Because of the different amounts of water in the glasses every glass is making a different sound when you hit it with the wooden stick. The sound tone depends on the sound vibrations, when you hit the glass with the most water in it, it has the lowest tone. More water means slower vibrations and a lower tone.

MOVING WATER MOLECULES

To perform the experiment you need a glass of cold water, glass of hot water, food coloring and an eye dropper.

Step by step
1. Equal the levels of hot water and cold water in the glasses
2. Put one drop of food coloring in both glasses (at the same time if possible)

Explanation
Because of the difference in the temperatures in water the food coloring will not spread through both glasses of water with the same speed. In the hot water are much faster molecules so the coloring will spread through it much faster than through the cold water.

FREEZING OIL AND WATER

To perform the experiment you need some water, a plastic container, cooking oil and a freezer.

Step by step
1. Pour some water in a container
2. Add some cooking oil in the water
3. Wait a few minutes (so the oil rises over the water)
4. Place the container in the freezer
5. Wait for a few hours

Explanation
Because the water changes its condition in the freezer from liquid to solid it replaces position with the oil. After a few hours in the freezer the oil will be under the water, because the water in solid condition is less dense than the oil.

AMPLIFY SOUND WITH A BALLOON

To perform the experiment you need a balloon.

Step by step
1. Inflate the balloon
2. Place the balloon close to your ear
3. Lightly tap on the side of the balloon (the opposite side where your ear is)

Explanation
Because of the air inside the balloon the sound that comes from tapping is much louder than it normally is. The molecules in the balloon are very close together, so they are a better conductor of sound waves than the normal air around you.

WHAT ABSORBS MORE HEAT?

To perform the experiment you need water, a thermometer, two identical glasses, two elastic bands, white paper and some black paper.

Step by step
1. Wrap the white paper around a glass
2. Put the elastic on the glass to hold the paper
3. Wrap the black paper around the other glass
4. Put the elastic on the glass to hold the paper
5. Fill both glasses with equal amount of water
6. Put the glasses out on the sun
7. Wait a few hours
8. Measure the temperature of the water in both glasses

Explanation
Because of the difference in the color of the paper the temperature of the water in the glass with black paper around it will be higher than the temperature of the water in the glass with white paper around it. The dark-colored objects absorb more light and heat than the light-colored objects, which reflect the light.

FLOATING PING PONG BALL

To perform the experiment you need a ping pong ball and a hair dryer.

Step by step
1. Turn on the hair dryer to a medium blow setting
2. Point the hair dryer straight up
3. Place the ping pong ball above the hair dryer

Explanation
Because of the airflow from the dryer the ping pong ball will calmly float over it. The hair dryer's airflow is pushing it up, at the same time the gravity is pushing it down. When the ball reaches balance between both forces it floats.

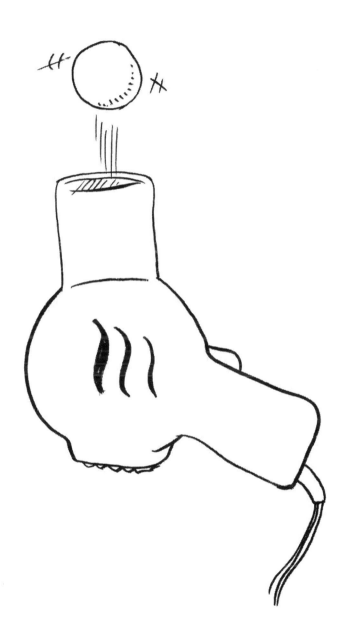

SINKING ORANGE

To perform the experiment you need an orange, container and water.

Step by step
1. Fill the container with water
2. Put the orange in the water (leave it in for a minute)
3. Take the orange out
4. Peel the orange
5. Put the orange back in the water

Explanation
Because of the its rind the orange will float when you put it in the water the first time. The rind is full of tiny air pockets which help the orange float in the water (because the density of the orange is lower than the density of the water). When you peel the rind of the orange sinks.

CRAZY PUTTY

To perform the experiment you need water, food coloring, one small container, one big container, PVA glue and a borax.

Step by step
1. Fill the bottom of the big container with PVA glue
2. Add in the glue a little water
3. Mix the water and the glue
4. Add a few drops of food coloring in the mixture
5. Mix the coloring and the mixture
6. Add a little borax in the mixture
7. Mix the mixture
8. Put the mixture in a small container

Explanation

Because of the ingredients you put in the mixture it will become a substance that you can squish or even bounce. When you mix the PVA glue and borax with water, the borax reacts with the glue molecules, joining them together in one big molecule. This becomes a putty like substance, which you can use to play with.

EGG IN A BOTTLE

To perform the experiment you need a hard-boiled egg, boiled water and a glass bottle (with the neck wide enough to sit the egg in). You need an adult to help you with this trick.

Step by step
1. Pour the boiled water into the bottle (half full)
2. Place the egg on the top of the glass (it has to sit in the neck of the glass)
3. Wait a few minutes

Explanation
Because of the difference of the temperature inside and outside the bottle the egg will be sucked into the bottle. As the warm air inside the bottle cools it creates a lower pressure than outside the bottle, so the greater pressure outside the bottle forces the egg into the bottle.

STATIC ELECTRICITY

To perform the experiment you need an aluminum can, two inflated balloons with string attached and a woolen fabric.

Step by step
1. Rub the two balloons one by one against the woolen fabric
2. Try to move the balloons together
3. Observe what happens
4. Rub the balloon on your hair
5. Slowly pull the balloon away from your hair
6. Observe what happens
7. Place the aluminum can on the table
8. Rub the balloon on your hair
9. Put the balloon near the can
10. Move the balloon
11. Observe what happen

Explanation

Because of the static electricity, you make with rubbing the balloons to the different things you can move the objects around. When you rub the balloon towards the other balloon or your hair you negatively charge it. when you put two negatively charged balloons together they are not attracted to each other and they don't want to be together. When you put negatively charged balloons next to positively charged aluminum can they attract each other (it works similar like with the magnets).

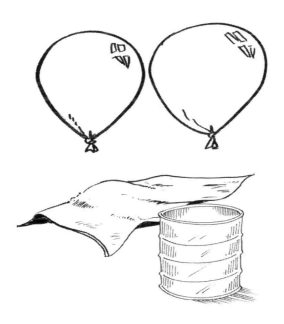

GRAVITY FREE WATER

To perform the experiment you need a glass of water (filled to the top) and a piece of cardboard.

Step by step
1. Place the cardboard over the mouth of the glass
2. Turn the glass upside down
3. Move away your hand that is holding the cardboard

Explanation
Because of the difference of the pressure level between outside and inside the glass you can make the water stand still in an upside-down turned glass. In the glass there is no air (only water) so the pressure in it is smaller than the pressure of the air outside the glass. This extra air pressure is holding the cardboard in place and the water inside the glass.

CUT ICE CUBES IN HALF

To perform the experiment you need an ice cube, container and a piece of fishing line with a weight tied to each end.

Step by step
1. Turn the container upside down
2. Place an ice cube on the top of the container
3. Put the fishing line over the ice cube (the weights are dangling on each side over the container)
4. Wait for a few minutes

Explanation
You can cut the ice cube on half because the pressure from each weight pulls string through the ice by melting the ice cube directly under the fishing line.

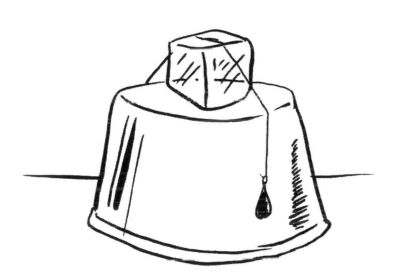

WHAT IS YOUR LUNG VOLUME?

To perform the experiment you need a large plastic bottle, water, kitchens sink and a clean plastic tube.

Step by step
1. Fill the bottle with water (to the top)
2. Put about 10 centimeters of water into the kitchen sink
3. Put your hand over the mouth of the bottle
4. Turn the bottle upside down
5. Put the mouth of the water under the water in the sink
6. Remove your hand off the bottle
7. Place one end of the plastic tube into the bottle
8. Breathe out through the tube as much you can
9. Measure the volume of the air your lungs breathed out

Explanation
Because you breathe air from your lungs through the tube into the bottle and that air replaces the extra water in the bottle, you can measure the volume of the air you breathed into the bottle. The air you breathe into the bottle will push some water from the bottle because there is no room for it. That is how you will know what your lung capacity is.

TORNADO IN A BOTTLE

To perform the experiment you need some water, glitter, dish detergent and a plastic bottle (with a stopper).

Step by step
1. Fill three quarters of the bottle with water
2. Add a few drops of dish detergent
3. Sprinkle in the water a few pinches of glitter
4. Put on a stopper (tightly)
5. Turn the bottle upside down
6. Hold the bottle by its neck
7. Quickly spin the bottle in circles

Explanation
Because of the spinning the bottle in a circular motion you will see a tornado like phenomenon in the middle of the bottle. The water is spinning around the center of the vortex due to centripetal force.

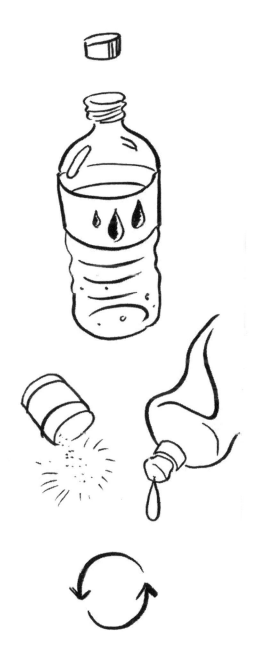

MAKING ICE

To perform the experiment you need a cup of cold water, cup of hot water, freezer and a timer.

Step by step
1. Place both cups with hot and cold water in the freezer
2. Check the cups every fifteen minutes

Explanation
Often iit happens that the hot water freezes before cold water! This phenomenon is known as the Mpemba effect. The scientists are still researching why is that so.

SPINNING BUCKET

To perform the experiment you need some water and a bucket.

Step by step
1. Fill the bucket with the water (half full)
2. Hold the bucket by its handle
3. Spin the bucket in circles

Explanation
Because of the spinning the bucket in a circular motion the water in the bucket will not get out of it. That happens because with your spinning a centripetal force is acting on the water and keeps it inside the bucket.

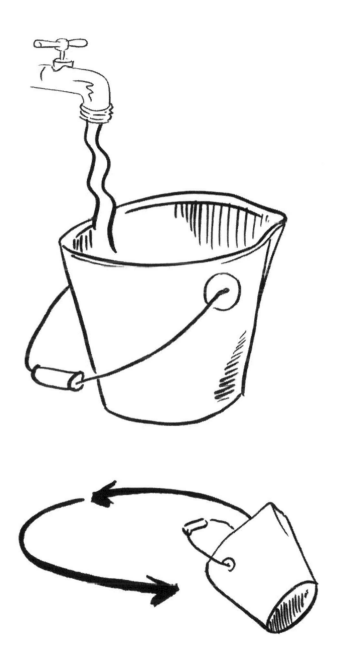

FAKE SNOT

To perform the experiment you need some boiling water, cup, corn syrup, gelatin, fork and a teaspoon.

Step by step
1. Fill the cup with a boiling water (half full)
2. Add three teaspoons of gelatin in the cup
3. Wait a minute
4. Stir the mixture with a fork
5. Add a little corn syrup
6. Stir the mixture with a fork
7. Slowly add more water (small amounts at the time)

Explanation
Because of the right ingredients you put in the mixture you can make yourself a fake snot. The snot is made of proteins and sugars. And the long strings in your mixture are protein stands, which makes snot sticky and capable to stretch.

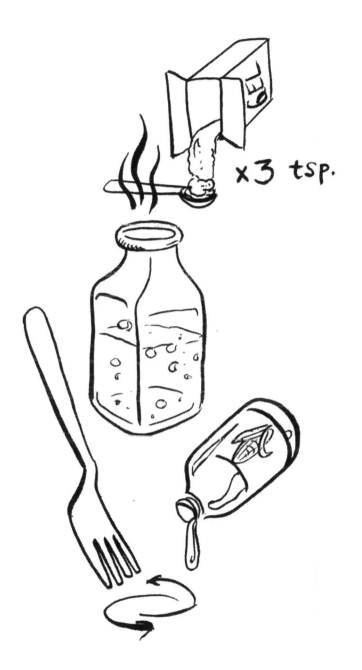

BLOWING UP BALLOONS WITH CO2

To perform the experiment you need a balloon, water, drinking straw, lemon juice, baking soda and a soft drinks bottle.

Step by step
1. Stretch the balloon (it will be easier to inflate it)
2. Pour 40 ml of water in the soft drinking bottle
3. Add a teaspoon of soda in the water
4. Stir the mixture with a straw (until the soda dissolve)
5. Pour the lemon juice in the mixture
6. Quickly place the balloon over the mouth of the bottle

Explanation
Because of the chemical reaction between the lemon juice and soda you can inflate the balloon just with placing it on the mouth of the bottle. When you mix lemon juice and soda they create a carbon dioxide (CO_2). The gas then goes up through the bottle mouth into the balloon, which instantly inflates.

INVISIBLE INK WITH LEMON JUICE

To perform the experiment you need water, half a lemon, spoon, bowl, cotton bud, white paper and a lamp.

Step by step
1. Squeeze the lemon into the bowl
2. Add few drops of water into the lemon juice
3. Dip the cotton bud in the mixture
4. Write a message with the cotton bud on the paper
5. Wait a few minutes
6. Hold the paper close to a lamp

Explanation
Because of the chemical structure of the lemon juice you can write secret messages with it. Lemon juice is very hard to notice when you put in on a white paper, but when you heat it, it will turn brown (because it oxidizes).

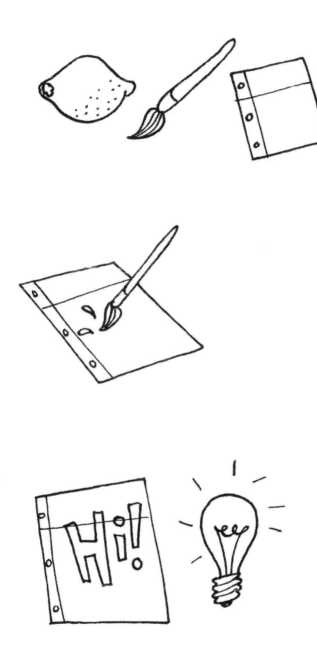

MAKE A LEMONADE FIZZY DRINK

To perform the experiment you need a lemon, water, drinking glass, baking soda and some sugar.

Step by step
1. Squeeze the lemon into the glass
2. Pour a water in the glass (same amount as the lemon juice)
3. Put a teaspoon of baking soda in the glass
4. Mix everything together
5. Try the mixture
6. Add some sugar if need to

Explanation
Because of the right ingredients, you put in the mixture you prepared a very good fizzy drink with lemon flavor. When mixing the lemon and soda you started a chemical reaction of which the result is creating the carbon dioxide. Carbon dioxide is the bubbles in soft drinks.

MAGNETIC ATTRACTION

To perform the experiment you need modelling clay, pencil (with an eraser) and a horseshoe magnet.

Step by step
1. Roll the modelling clay into a ball (the size of a fist)
2. Push the pencil into the clay so it stands upright (the eraser end of pencil)
3. Balance the horseshoe magnet above the pencil lead

Explanation
Because of the earth's magnetic field which attracts the magnet on the pencil, the magnet will slowly move in a north-south direction. It works the same like the compass.

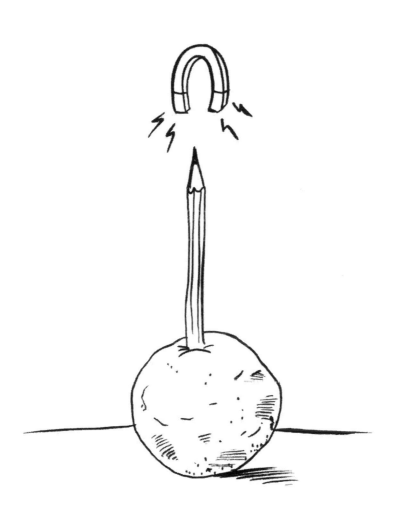

WILL THE ICE MELT AND OVERFLOW?

To perform the experiment you need a glass of warm water and an ice cube.

Step by step
1. Slowly put the ice cube into the warm water
2. Observe the water level as the ice cube melts

Explanation
Because the water takes up more space when it freezes than it does in a liquid state you will see that the level of the water in the glass will get lower as the ice cube melts down.

MAKE RAIN

To perform the experiment, you need some water, a saucepan, ice cubes and a pair of oven mitts.

Step by step
1. Ask an adult for help
2. Boil some water in the saucepan
3. Put on the oven mitts
4. Take ice cubes and hold them over the steam from the saucepan

Explanation
The steam from the boiling water in the saucepan changes the ice cubes back into a liquid water. Ice cubes are melting, so the drops are falling down – it looks like it is raining.

Manufactured by Amazon.ca
Bolton, ON